I0478695

GREECE

PHOTOGRAPHS BY ELIZABETH KRAMER

THIS IS PART OF THE VISITING SERIES.

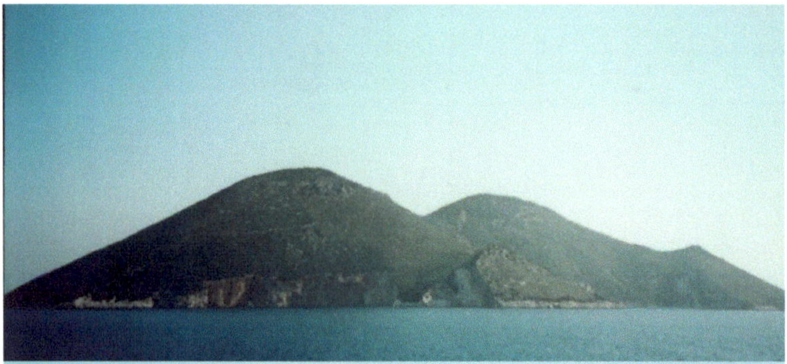

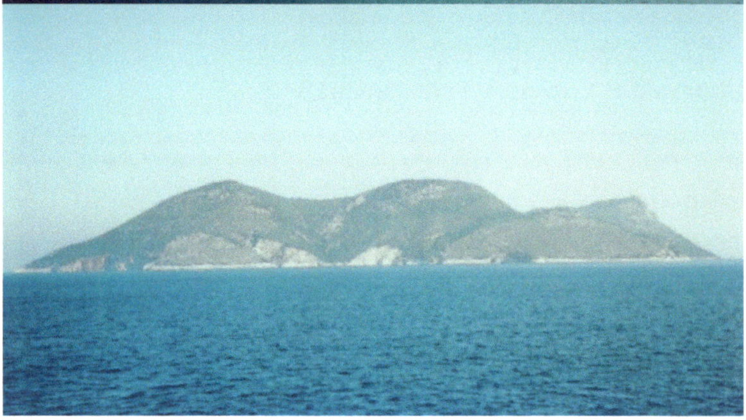

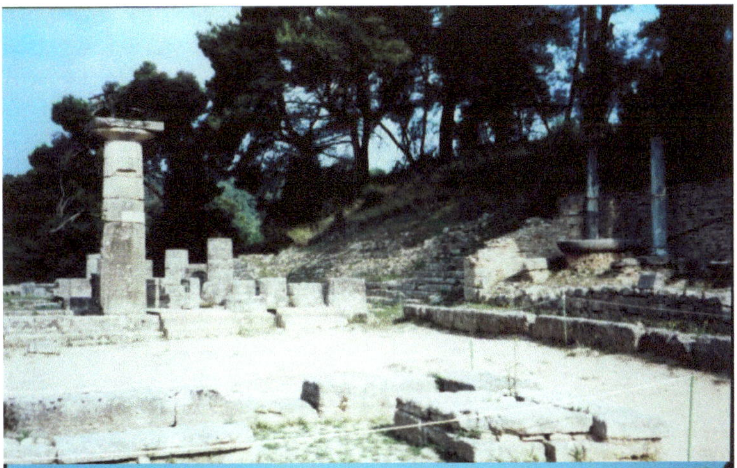
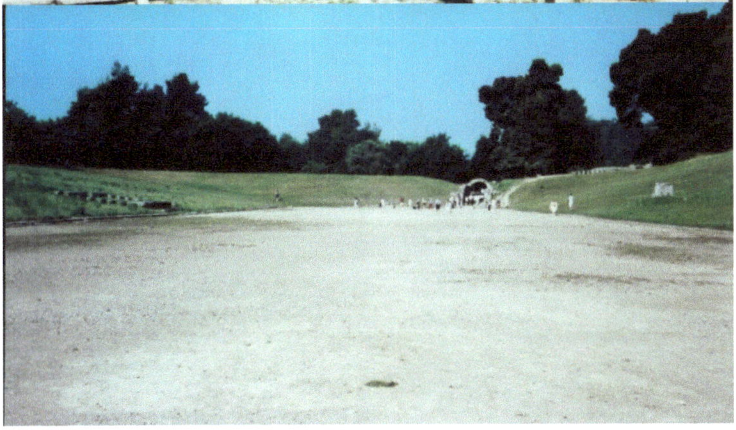

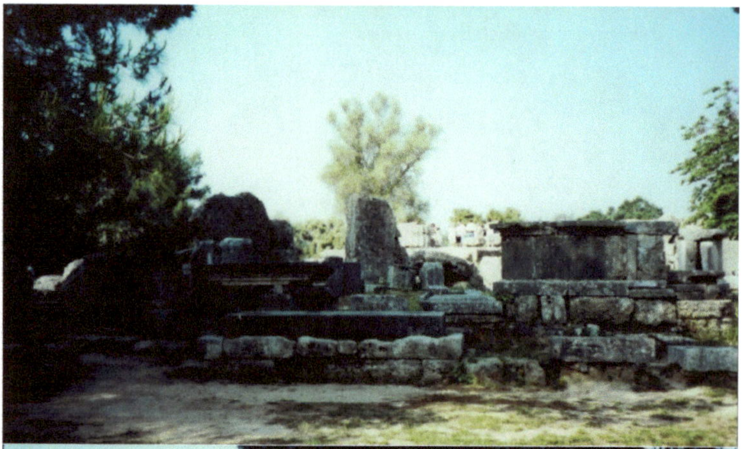

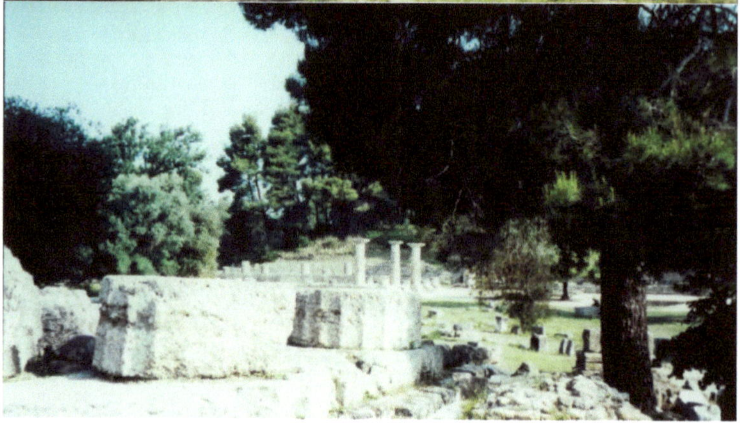

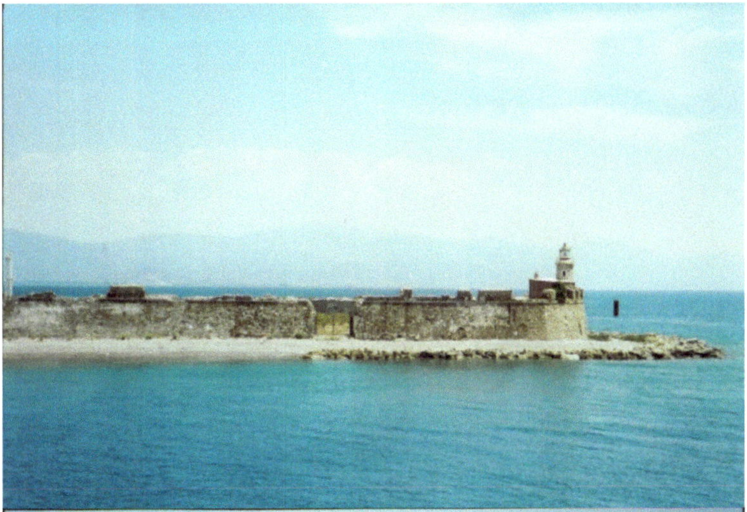

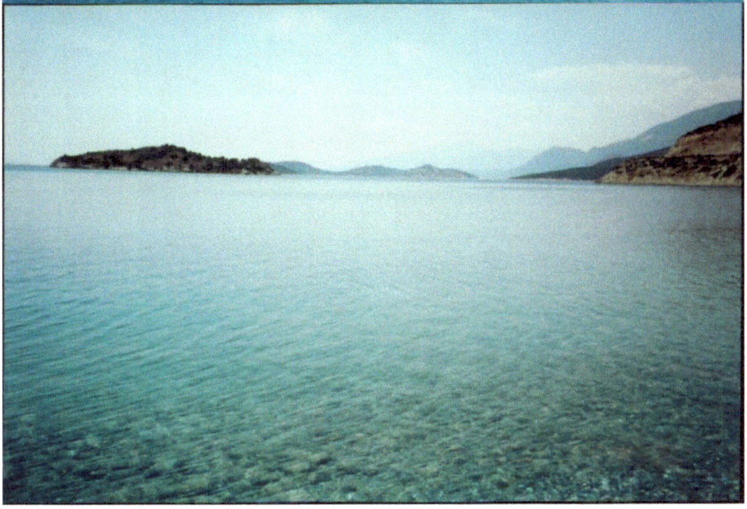

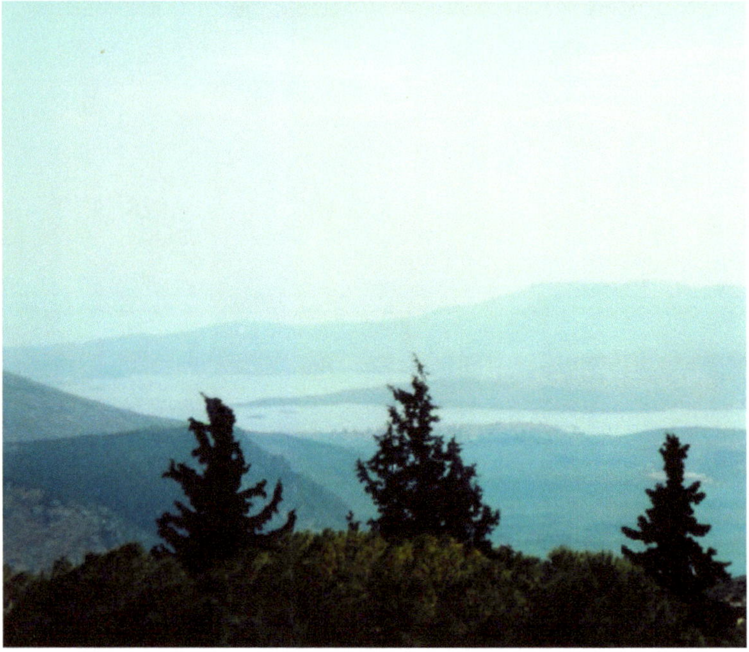

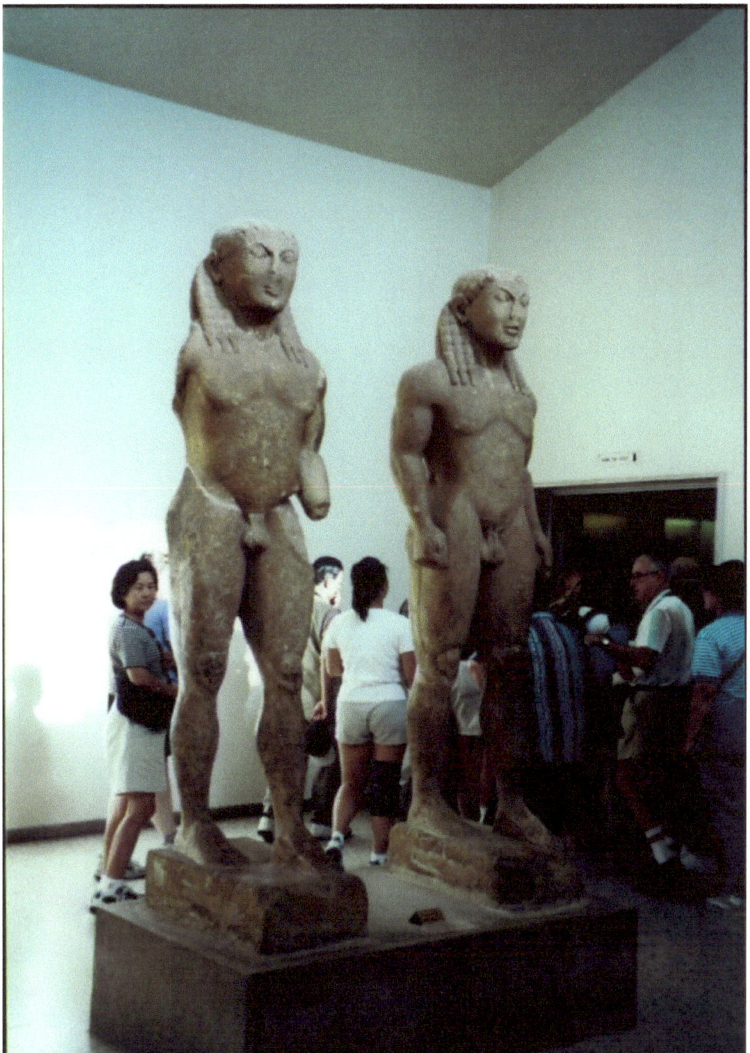

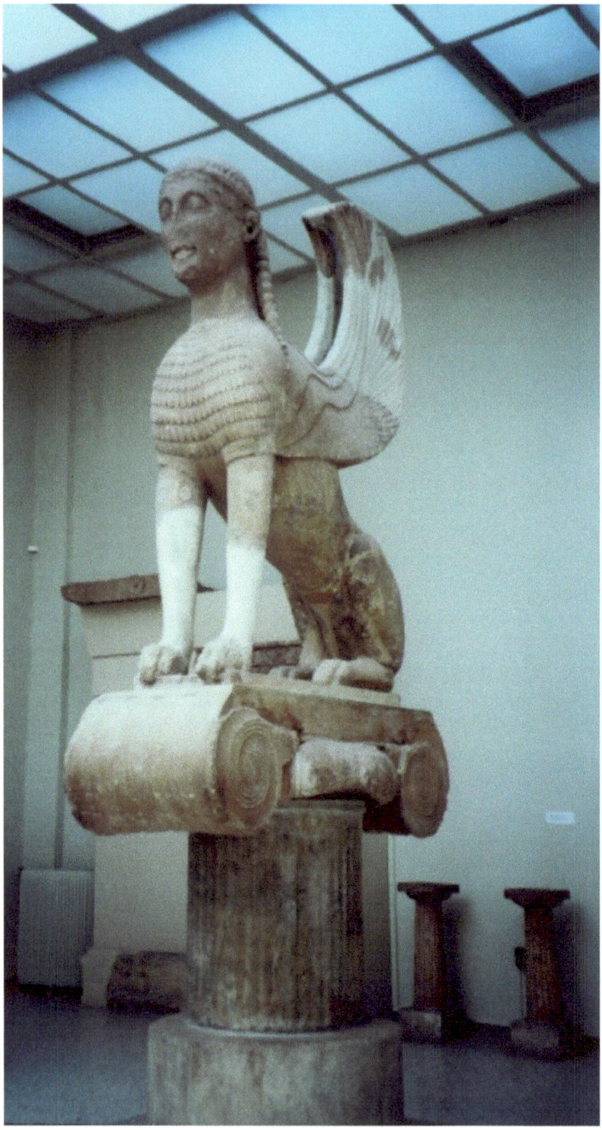

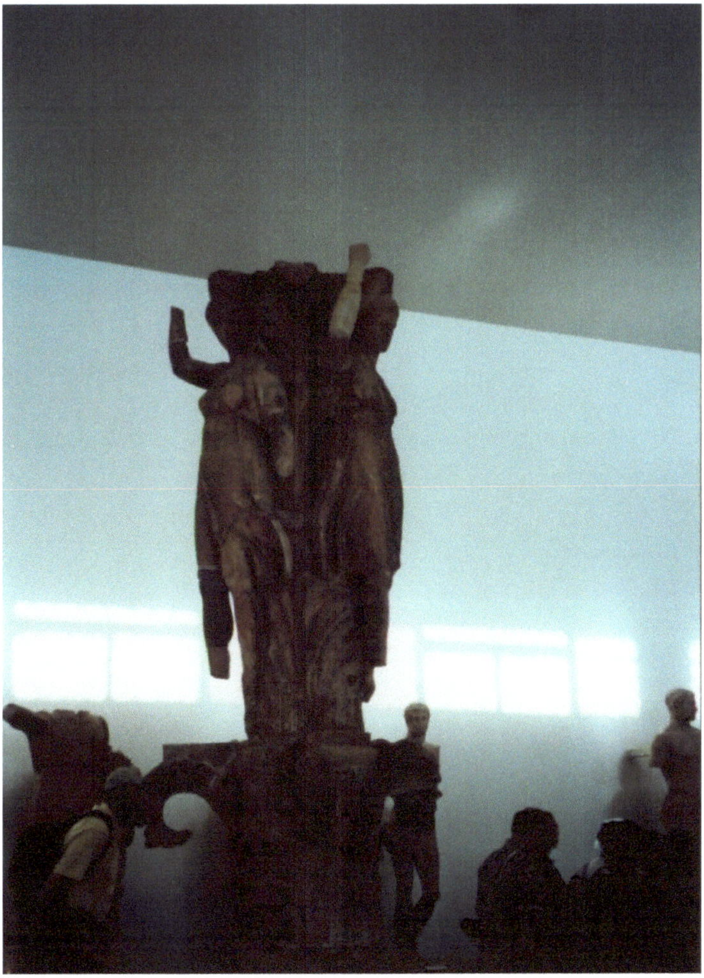

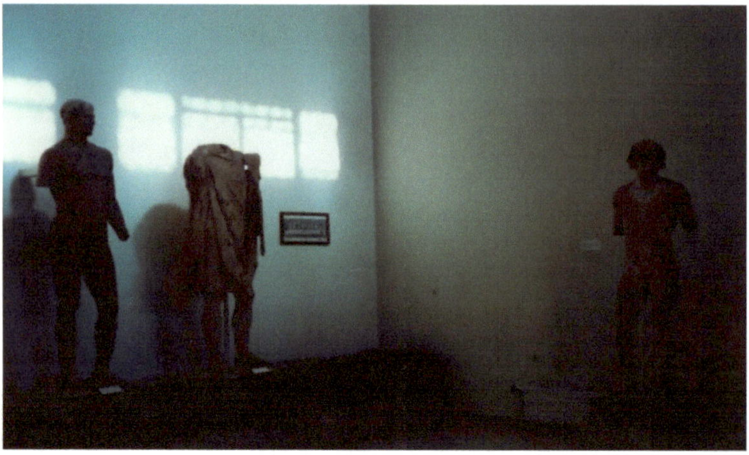

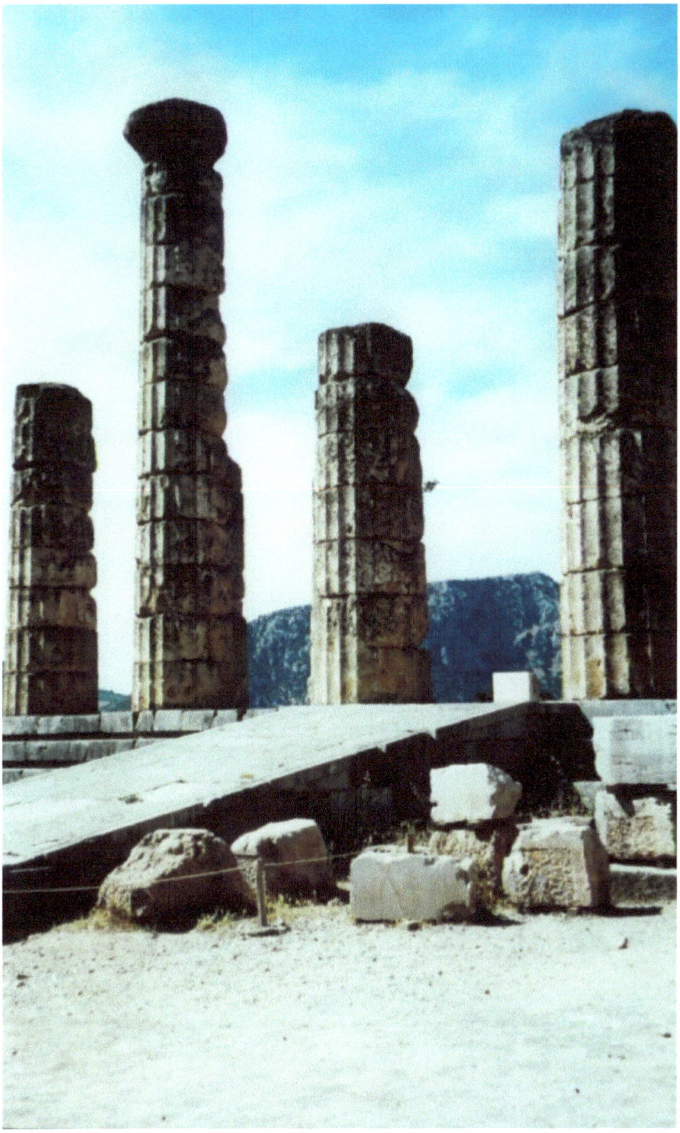

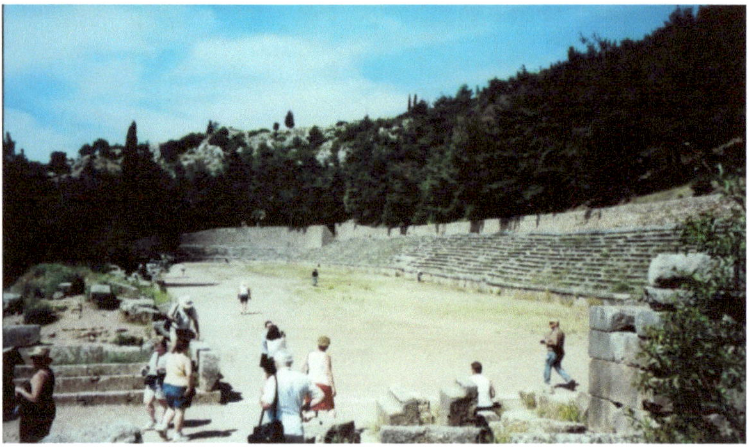

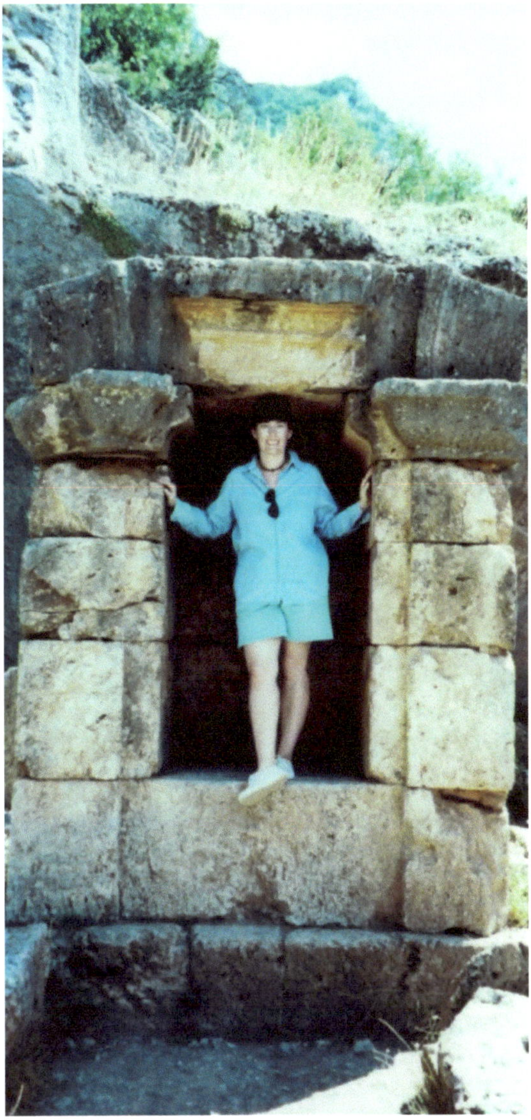

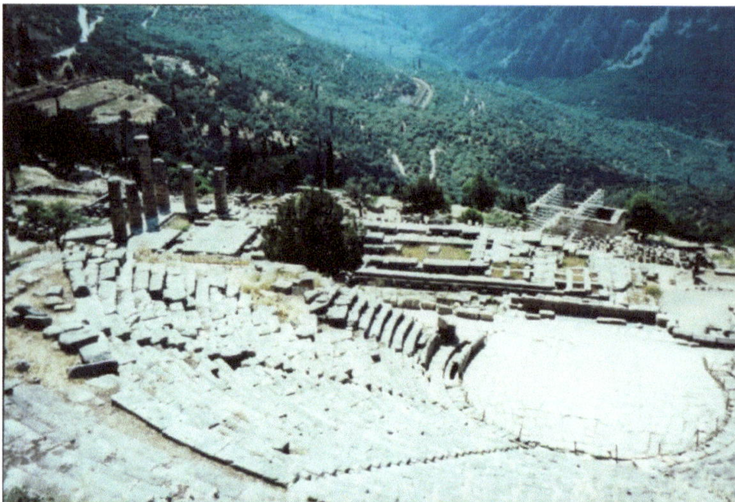

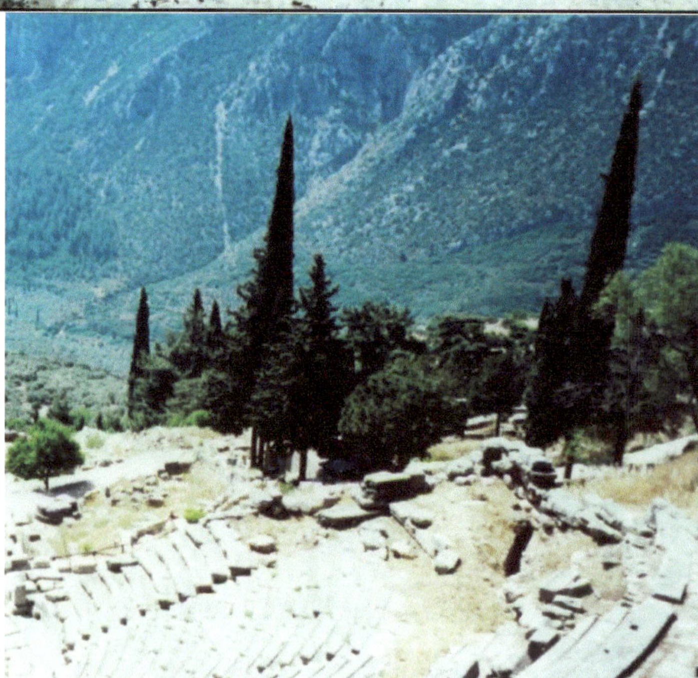

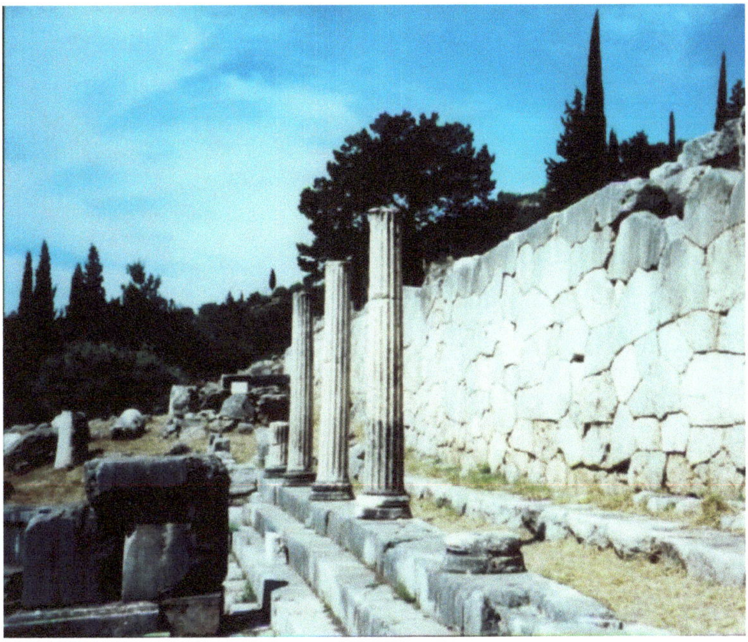

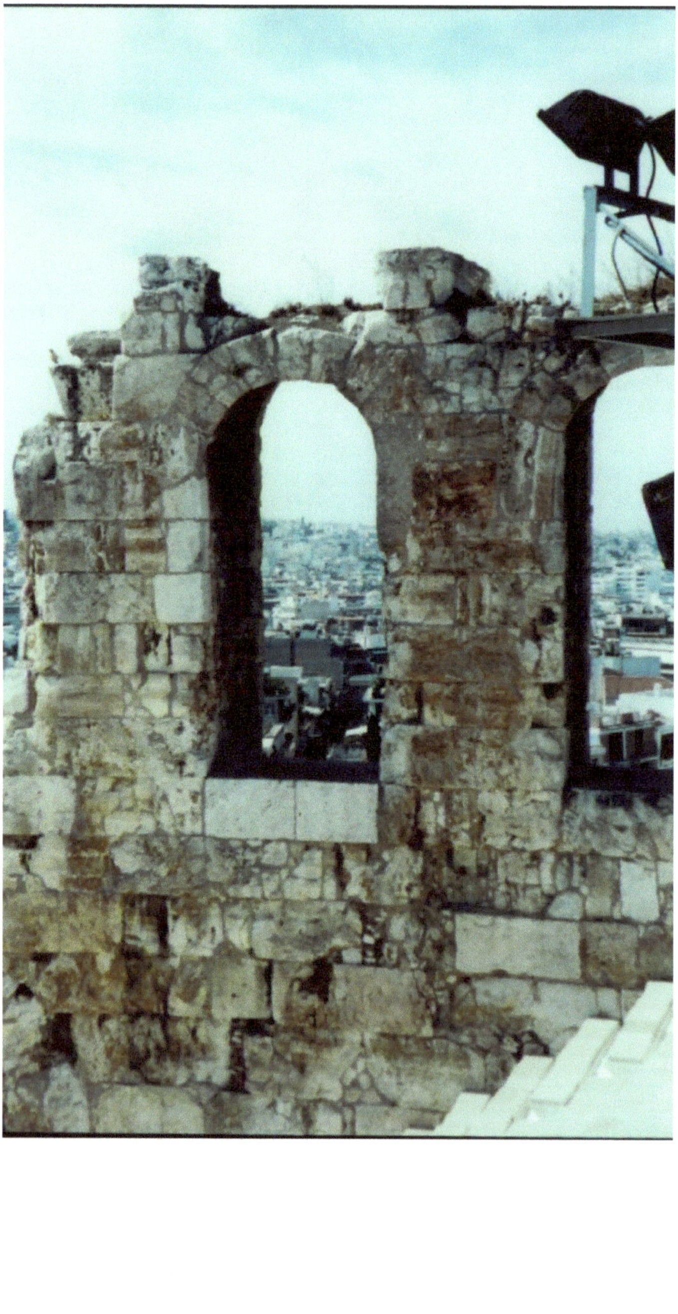

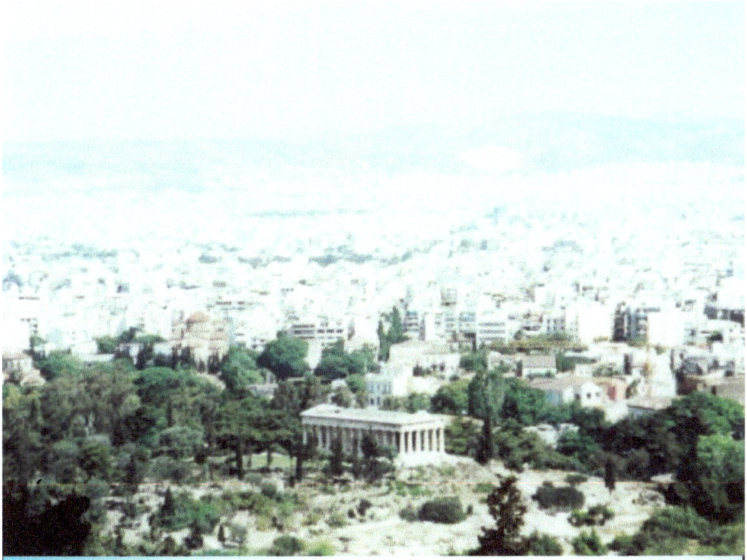

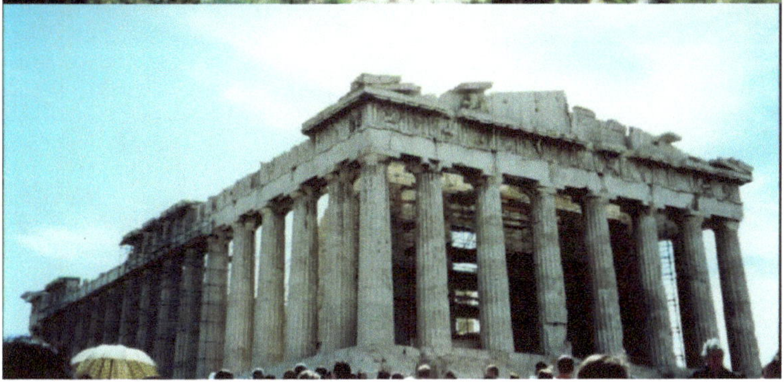

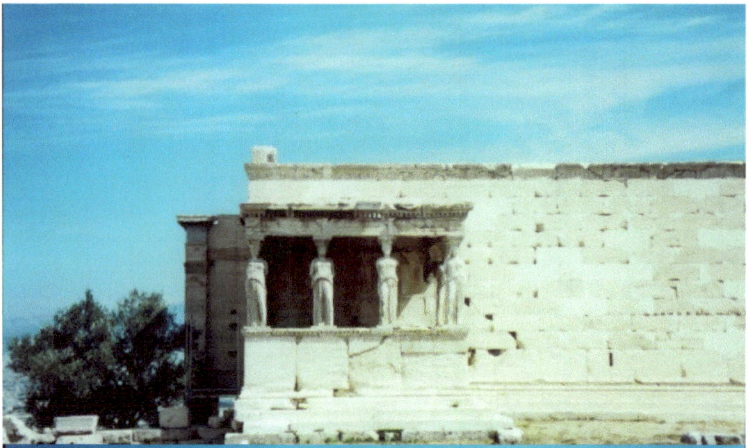
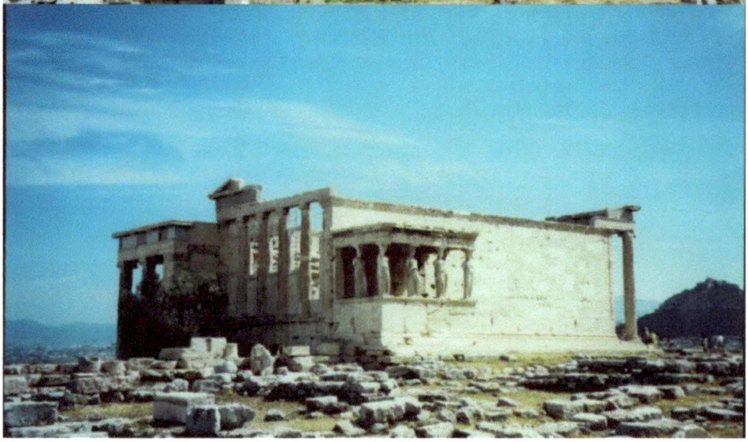

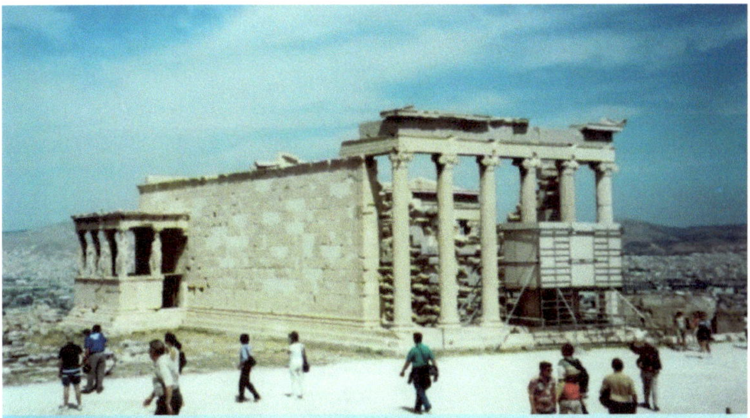

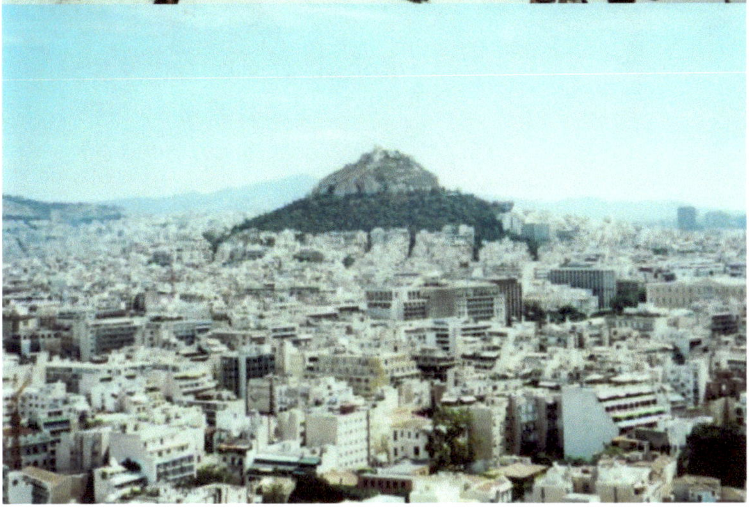

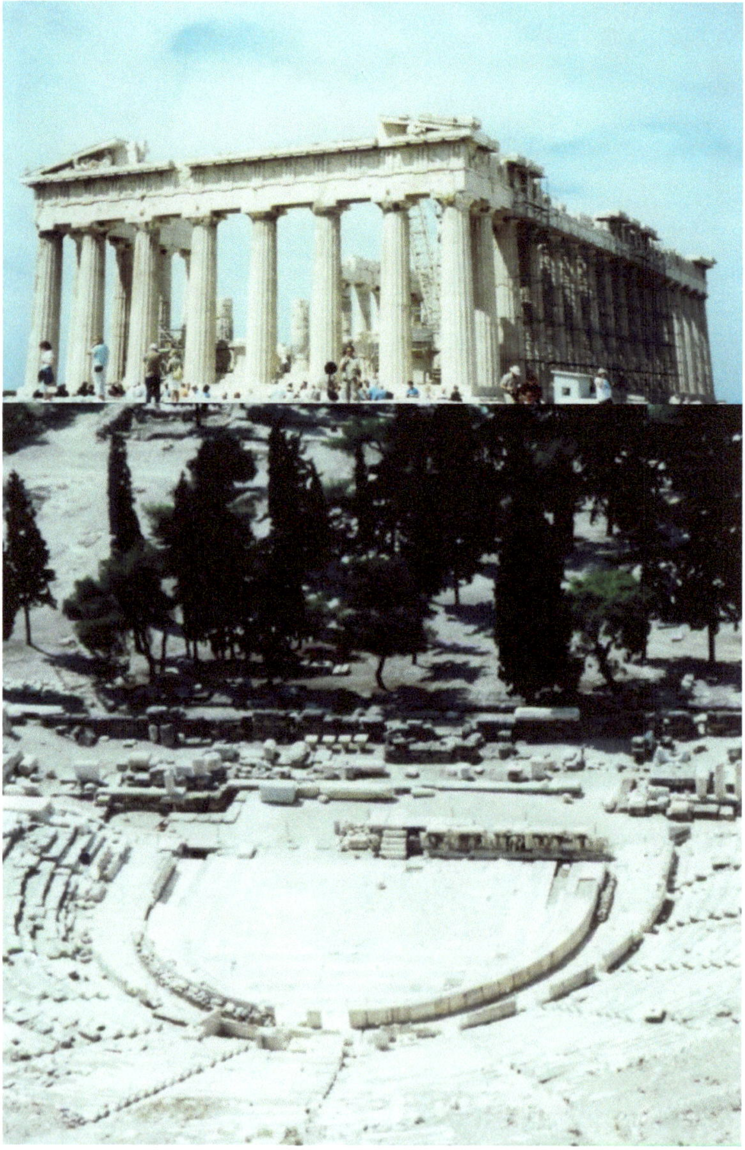

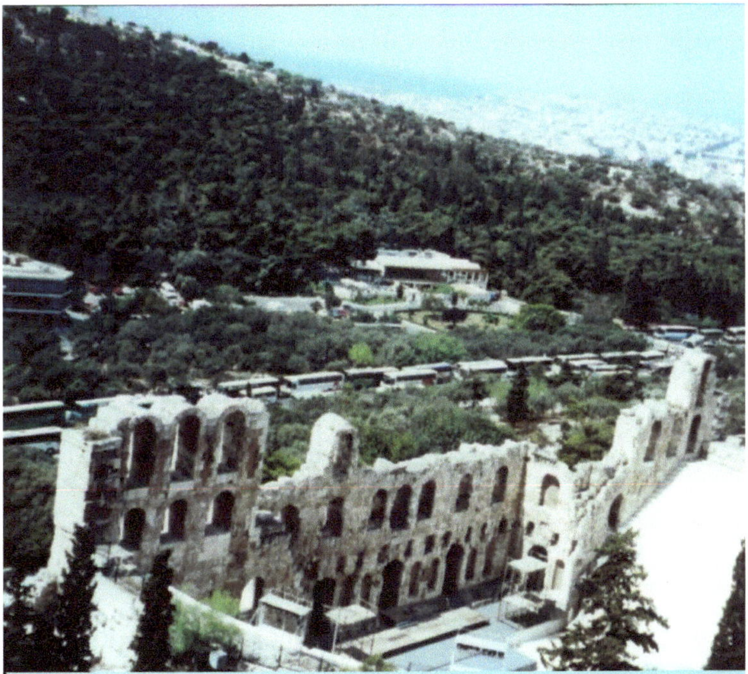

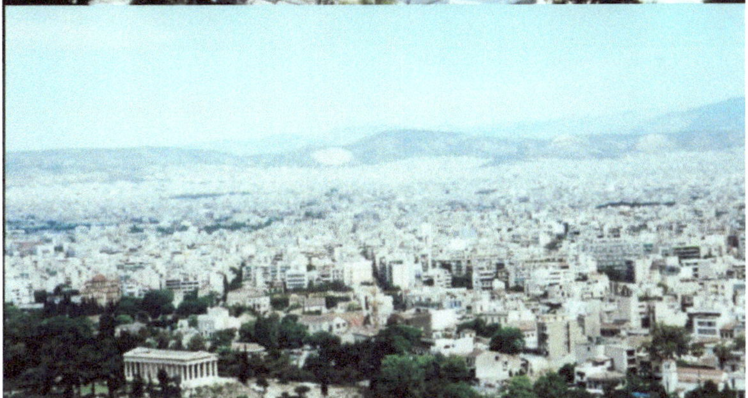

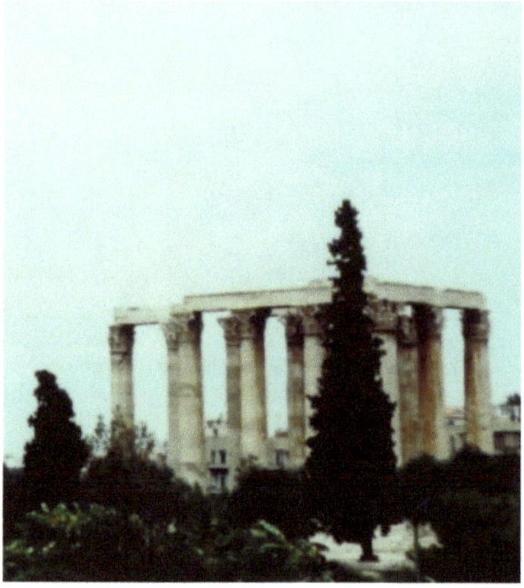

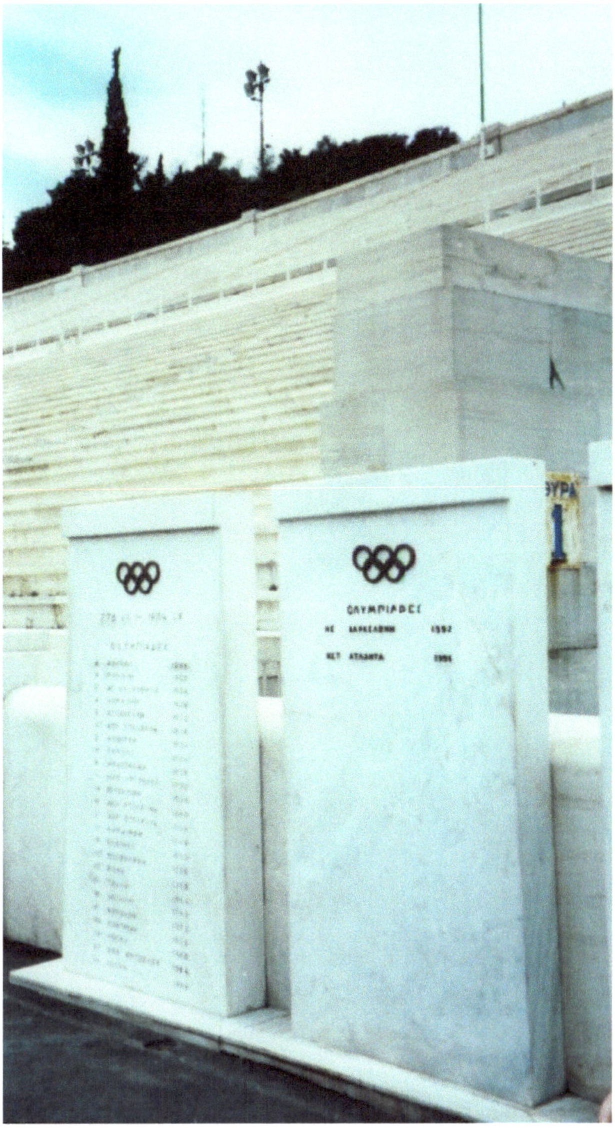
ΟΛΥΜΠΙΑΔΕΣ

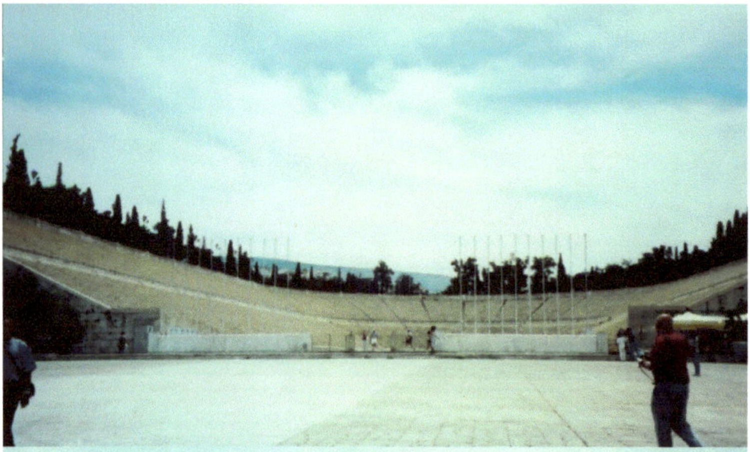

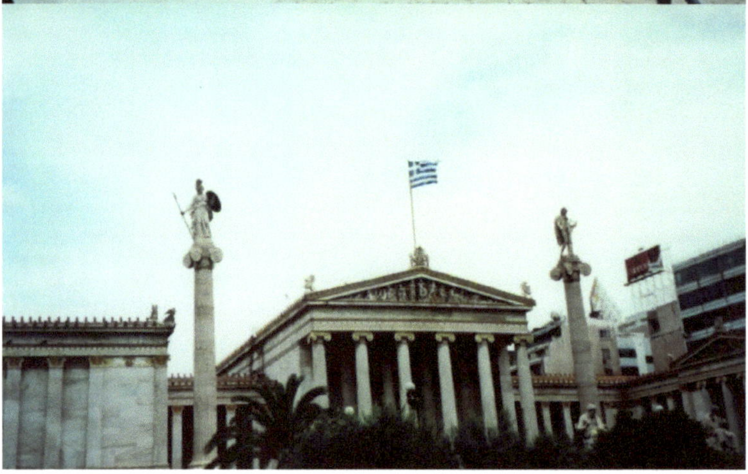

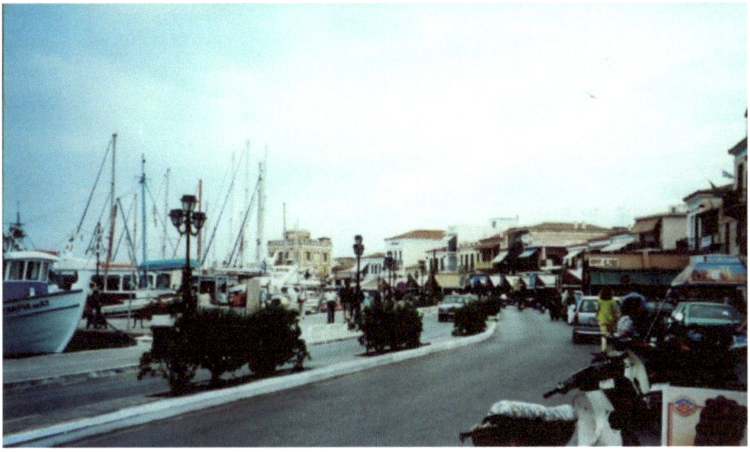

www.ingramcontent.com/pod-product-compliance
Lightning Source LLC
Chambersburg PA
CBHW041620180526
45159CB00002BC/949
* 9 7 8 1 5 1 4 8 2 7 1 6 1 *